RUDOLF STEINER (1861–1925) called his spiritual philosophy 'anthroposophy', meaning 'wisdom of the human being'. As a highly developed seer, he based his work on direct knowledge and perception of spiritual dimensions. He initiated a modern and universal 'science of spirit', accessible to anyone willing to exercise clear and unprejudiced thinking.

From his spiritual investigations Steiner provided suggestions for the renewal of many activities, including education (both general and special), agriculture, medicine, economics, architecture, science, philosophy, religion and the arts. Today there are thousands of schools, clinics, farms and other organizations involved in practical work based on his principles. His many published works feature his research into the spiritual nature of the human being, the evolution of the world and humanity, and methods of personal development. Steiner wrote some 30 books and delivered over 6000 lectures across Europe. In 1924 he founded the General Anthroposophical Society, which today has branches throughout the world.

RUDOLF STEINER

HUMAN and COSMIC THOUGHT

Four lectures given in Berlin
from 20th to 23rd January, 1914
during the Second General Meeting
of the Anthroposophical Society

Translation revised by Charles Davy

RUDOLF STEINER PRESS

Rudolf Steiner Press,
Hillside House, The Square
Forest Row, RH18 5ES

www.rudolfsteinerpress.com

First published by Rudolf Steiner Press 1961
Reprinted 1991, 2015

Originally published in German under the title *Der menschliche und der kosmische Gedanke* (volume 151 in the *Rudolf Steiner Gesamtausgabe* or Collected Works) by Rudolf Steiner Verlag, Dornach. Based on shorthand reports unrevised by the speaker. This authorized translation is based on the fourth edition, 1961

Published by permission of the Rudolf Steiner Nachlassverwaltung, Dornach

A CIP catalogue record for this book is available from the British Library

ISBN 978 1 85584 416 2

Cover by Morgan Creative
Typeset by DP Photosetting, Neath, West Glamorgan
Printed and bound by 4Edge Ltd., Essex

The following lectures were given by Rudolf Steiner to an audience familiar with the background and fundamental principles of his anthroposophical teaching. In his autobiography, *The Course of my Life*, he emphasises the distinction between his written works on the one hand and, on the other, reports (not personally revised by him) of lectures which were given as oral communications and were not originally intended for print. For an intelligent appreciation of the lectures—and especially in the case of those printed here—it should be borne in mind that certain premises were taken for granted when the words were spoken. "These premises," Rudolf Steiner writes, "include at the very least, the anthroposophical knowledge of Man and of the Cosmos in its spiritual essence, also what may be called 'anthroposophical history', told as an outcome of research into the spiritual world."

CONTENTS

LECTURE ONE

IN THESE four lectures which I am giving in the course of our General Meeting, I should like to speak from a particular standpoint about the connection between Man and the Cosmos. I will first indicate what this standpoint is.

Man experiences within himself what we may call thought, and in thought he can feel himself directly active, able to exercise his activity. When we observe anything external, e.g. a rose or a stone, and picture it to ourselves, someone may rightly say: "You can never know how much of the stone or the rose you have really got hold of when you imagine it. You see the rose, its external red colour, its form, and how it is divided into single petals; you see the stone with its colour, with its several corners, but you must always say to yourself that hidden within it there may be something else which does not appear to you externally. You do not know how much of the rose or of the stone your mental picture of it embraces."

But when someone has a thought, then it is he himself who makes the thought. One might say that he is within every fibre of his thought, a complete participator in its activity. He knows: "Everything that is in the thought I have thought into it, and what I have not thought into it cannot be within it. I survey the thought. Nobody can say, when I set a thought before my mind, that there may still be something more in the thought, as there may be in the rose and in the stone, for I have myself engendered the thought and am present in it, and so I know what is in it."

In truth, thought is most completely our possession. If we can find the relation of thought to the Cosmos, to the Universe, we shall find the relation to the Cosmos of what is most completely ours. This can assure us that we have here a fruitful standpoint from which to observe the relation of man to the universe. We will therefore embark on this course; it will lead us to significant heights of anthroposophical observation.

In the present lecture we shall have to prepare a groundwork which may perhaps appear to many of you as somewhat abstract. But later on we shall see that we need this groundwork and that

9

without it we could approach only with a certain superficiality the high goals we shall be striving to attain.

We can thus start from the conviction that when man holds to that which he possesses in his thought, he can find an intimate relation of his being to the Cosmos. But in starting from this point of view we do encounter a difficulty, a great difficulty—not for our understanding but in practice. For it is indeed true that a man lives within every fibre of his thought, and therefore must be able to know his thought more intimately than he can know any perceptual image, but—yes—most people have no thoughts! And as a rule this is not thoroughly realised, for the simple reason that one must have thoughts in order to realise it. What hinders people in the widest circles from having thoughts is that for the ordinary requirements of life they have no need to go as far as thinking; they can get along quite well with words. Most of what we call "thinking" in ordinary life is merely a flow of words: people think in words, and much more often than is generally supposed. Many people, when they ask for an explanation of something, are satisfied if the reply includes some word with a familiar ring, reminding them of this or that. They take the feeling of familiarity for an explanation and then fancy they have grasped the thought.

Indeed, this very tendency led at a certain time in the evolution of intellectual life to an outlook which is still shared by many persons who call themselves "thinkers". For the new edition of my *Welt- und Lebensanschauungen im neunzehnten Jahrhundert* (Views of the World and of Life in the Nineteenth Century)* I tried to rearrange the book quite thoroughly, first by prefacing it with an account of the evolution of Western thought from the sixth century B.C. up to the nineteenth century A.D., and then by adding to the original conclusion a description of spiritual life in terms of thinking up to our own day. The

* First published (two volumes) in Berlin, 1900-1. In 1914 the contents were recast and published in a different form as *Die Rätsel der Philosophie* (Riddles of Philosophy). The fourth edition is included in the Complete Edition of Rudolf Steiner's work. (Rudolf Steiner Nachlassverwaltung, Dornach, Switzerland.)

content of the book has also been rearranged in many ways, for I have tried to show how thought as we know it really appeared first in a certain specific period. One might say that it first appeared in the sixth or eighth century B.C. Before then the human soul did not at all experience what can be called "thought" in the true sense of the word. What did human souls experience previously? They experienced pictures; all their experience of the external world took the form of pictures. I have often spoken of this from certain points of view. This picture-experience is the last phase of the old clairvoyant experience. After that, for the human soul, the "picture" passes over into "thought".

My intention in this book was to bring out this finding of Spiritual Science purely by tracing the course of philosophic evolution. Strictly on this basis, it is shown that thought was born in ancient Greece, and that as a human experience it sprang from the old way of perceiving the external world in pictures. I then tried to show how thought evolves further in Socrates, Plato, Aristotle; how it takes certain forms; how it develops further; and then how, in the Middle Ages, it leads to something of which I will now speak.

The development of thought leads to a stage of doubting the existence of what are called "universals", general concepts, and thus to so-called Nominalism, the view that universals can be no more than "names", nothing but words. And this view is still widely held to-day.

In order to make this clear, let us take a general concept that is easily observable—the concept "triangle". Now anyone still in the grip of Nominalism of the eleventh to the thirteenth centuries will say somewhat as follows: "Draw me a triangle!" Good! I will draw a triangle for him:

"Right!" says he, "that is a quite specific triangle with three acute angles. But I will draw you another." And he draws a right-angled triangle, and another with an obtuse angle.

Then says the person in question: "Well, now we have an acute-angled triangle, a right-angled triangle and an obtuse-angled triangle. They certainly exist. But they are not *the* triangle. The collective or general triangle must contain everything that a triangle can contain. But a triangle that is acute-angled cannot be at the same time right-angled and obtuse-angled. Hence there cannot be a collective triangle, 'Collective' is an expression that includes the specific triangles, but a general concept of the triangle does not exist. It is a word that embraces the single details."

Naturally, this goes further. Let us suppose that someone says the word "lion". Anyone who takes his stand on the basis of Nominalism may say: "In the Berlin Zoo there is a lion; in the Hanover Zoo there is also a lion; in the Munich Zoo there is still another. There are these single lions, but there is no general lion connected with the lions in Berlin, Hanover and Munich; that is a mere word which embraces the single lions." There are only separate things; and beyond the separate things—so says the Nominalist—we have nothing but words that comprise the separate things.

As I have said, this view is still held to-day by many clear-thinking logicians. And anyone who tries to explain all this will really have to admit: "There *is* something strange about it; without going further in some way I can't make out whether there really is or is not this 'lion-in-general' and the 'triangle-in-general'. I find it far from clear." And now suppose someone came along and said: "Look here, my dear chap, I can't let you off with just showing me the Berlin or Hanover or Munich lion.

If you declare that there is a lion-in-general, then you must take me somewhere where it exists. If you show me only the Berlin, Hanover, or Munich lion, you have not proved to me that a 'lion-in-general' exists." . . . If someone were to come along who held this view, and if you had to show him the "lion-in-general", you would be in a difficulty. It is not so easy to say where you would have to take him.

We will not go on just yet to what we can learn from Spiritual Science; that will come in time. For the moment we will remain at the point which can be reached by thinking only, and we shall have to say to ourselves: "On *this* ground, we cannot manage to lead any doubter to the 'lion-in-general'. It really can't be done." Here we meet with one of the difficulties which we simply have to admit. For if we refuse to recognise this difficulty in the domain of ordinary thought, we shall not admit the difficulty of human cognition in general.

Let us keep to the triangle, for it makes no difference to the thing-in-general whether we clarify the question by means of the triangle, the lion, or something else. At first it seems hopeless to think of drawing a triangle that would contain all characteristics, all triangles. And because it not only seems hopeless, but *is* hopeless for ordinary human thinking, therefore all conventional philosophy stands here at a boundary-line, and its task should be to make a proper acknowledgment that, as conventional philosophy, it does stand at a boundary-line. But this applies only to conventional philosophy. There is a possibility of passing beyond the boundary, and with this possibility we will now make ourselves acquainted.

Let us suppose that we do not draw the triangle so that we simply say: Now I have drawn you a triangle, and here it is:

In that case the objection could always be raised that it is an acute-angled triangle; it is not a general triangle. The triangle *can* be drawn differently. Properly speaking it *cannot*, but we shall soon see how this "can" and "cannot" are related to one another. Let us take this triangle that we have here, and let us allow each side to move as it will in any direction, and moreover we allow it to move with varying speeds, so that next moment the sides take, e.g., these positions:

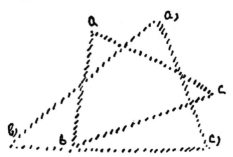

In short, we arrive at the uncomfortable notion of saying: I will not only draw a triangle and let it stay as it is, but I will make certain demands on your imagination. You must think to yourself that the sides of the triangle are in continual motion. When they are in motion, then out of the form of the movements there can arise simultaneously a right-angled, or an obtuse-angled triangle, or any other.

In this field we can do and also require two different things. We can first make it all quite easy; we draw a triangle and have done with it. We know how it looks and we can rest comfortably in our thoughts, for we have got what we want. But we can also take the triangle as a starting-point, and allow each side to move in various directions and at different speeds. In this case it is not quite so easy; we have to carry out movements in our thought. But in this way we really do lay hold of the triangle in its general form; we fail to get there only if we are content with *one* triangle. The general thought, "triangle", is there if we keep the thought in continual movement, if we make it versatile.

This is just what the philosophers have never done; they have not set their thoughts into movement. Hence they are brought to a halt at a boundary-line, and they take refuge in Nominalism.

We will now translate what I have just been saying into a language that we know, that we have long known. If we are to rise from the specific thought to the general thought, we have to bring the specific thought into motion; thus thought in movement becomes the "general thought" by passing constantly from one form into another. "Form", I say; rightly understood, this means that the whole is in movement, and each entity brought forth by the movement is a self-contained form. Previously I drew only single forms: an acute-angled, a right-angled, and an obtuse-angled triangle. Now I am drawing something—as I said, I do not really draw it—but you can picture to yourselves what the idea is meant to evoke—the general thought is in motion, and brings forth the single forms as its stationary states.

"Forms", I said—hence we see that the philosophers of Nominalism, who stand before a boundary-line, go about their work in a certain realm, the realm of the Spirits of Form. Within this realm, which is all around us, forms dominate; and therefore in this realm we find separate, strictly self-contained forms. The philosophers I mean have never made up their minds to go outside this realm of forms, and so, in the realm of universals, they can recognise nothing but words, veritably mere words. If they were to go beyond the realm of specific entities—i.e. of forms—they would find their way to mental pictures which are in continual motion; that is, in their thinking they would come to a realisation of the realm of the Spirits of Movement—the next higher Hierarchy. But these philosophers will not condescend to that. And when in recent times a Western thinker did consent to think correctly in this way, he was little understood, although much was said and much nonsense talked about him. Turn to what Goethe wrote in his "Metamorphosis of Plants" and see what he called the "primal plant" (*Urpflanze*), and then turn to what he called the "primal animal" (*Urtier*) and you will find that you can understand these concepts "primal plant" and "primal animal" only if your thoughts are mobile—when you think in mobile terms. If you accept this mobility, of which Goethe himself speaks, you are not stuck with an isolated concept bounded by fixed forms. You have the living element which ramifies through the whole evolution of the animal kingdom, or the plant-kingdom, and creates the forms. During this process it changes—as the triangle changes into an acute-angled or an obtuse-angled one—becoming now "wolf", now "lion", now "beetle", in accordance with the metamorphoses of its mobility during its passage through the particular entities. Goethe brought the petrified formal concepts into movement. That was his great central act; his most significant contribution to the nature-study of his time.

You see here an example of how Spiritual Science is in fact adapted to leading men out of the fixed assumptions to which they cannot help clinging to-day, even if they are philosophers. For without concepts gained through Spiritual Science it is not possible, if one is sincere, to concede that general categories can be anything more than "mere words". That is why I said that most people have no real thoughts, but merely a flow of words, and if one speaks to them of thoughts, they reject it.

When does one speak to people of "thoughts"? When, for example, one says that animals have Group-souls. For it amounts to the same whether one says "collective thoughts" or "group-souls" (we shall see in the course of these lectures what the connection is between the two). But the Group-soul cannot be understood except by thinking of it as being in motion, in continual external and internal motion; otherwise one does not come to the Group-soul. But people reject that. Hence they reject the Group-soul, and equally the collective thought.

For getting to know the outside world you need no thoughts; you need only a remembrance of what you have seen in the kingdom of form. That is all most people know, and for them, accordingly, general thoughts remain mere words. And if among the many different Spirits of the higher Hierarchies there were not the Genius of Speech—who forms general words for general concepts—men themselves would not come to it. Thus their first ideas of things-in-themselves come to men straight out of language itself, and they know very little about such ideas except in so far as language preserves them.

16

We can see from this that there must be something peculiar about the thinking of real thoughts. And this will not surprise us if we realise how difficult it really is for men to attain to clarity in the realm of thought. In ordinary, external life, when a person wants to brag a little, he will often say that "thinking is easy". But it is not easy, for real thinking always demands a quite intimate, though in a certain sense unconscious, impulse from the realm of the Spirits of Movement. If thinking were so very easy, then such colossal blunders would not be made in the region of thought. Thus, for more than a century now, people have worried themselves over a thought I have often mentioned—a thought formulated by Kant.

Kant wanted to drive out of the field the so-called "ontological proof of God". This ontological proof of God dates from the time of Nominalism, when it was said that nothing general existed which corresponded to general or collective thoughts, as single, specific objects correspond to specific thoughts. The argument says, roughly: If we presuppose God, then He must be an absolutely perfect Being. If He is an absolutely perfect Being, then He must not lack "being", i.e. existence, for otherwise there would be a still more perfect Being who would possess those attributes one has in mind, and would also exist. Thus one must think that the most perfect Being actually exists. One cannot conceive of God as otherwise than existing, if one thinks of Him as the most perfect Being. That is: out of the concept itself one can deduce that, according to the ontological proof, there must be God.

Kant tried to refute this proof by showing that out of a "concept" one could not derive the existence of a thing, and for this he coined the famous saying I have often mentioned: A hundred *actual* thalers are not less and not more than a hundred *possible* thalers. That is, if a thaler has three hundred pfennigs, then for each one of a hundred possible thalers one must reckon three hundred pfennigs: and in like manner three hundred pfennigs for each of a hundred actual thalers. Thus a hundred possible thalers contain just as much as a hundred actual thalers, i.e. it makes no difference whether I *think* of a hundred actual or a hundred possible thalers. Hence one may not derive existence from the

17

mere thought of an absolutely perfect Being, because the mere thought of a possible God would have the same attributes as the thought of an actual God.

That appears very reasonable. And yet for a century people have been worrying themselves as to how it is with the hundred possible and the hundred actual thalers. But let us take a very obvious point of view, that of practical life; can one say from this point of view that a hundred actual thalers do not contain more than a hundred possible ones? One can say that a hundred actual thalers contain exactly a hundred thalers more than do a hundred possible ones! And it is quite clear: if you think of a hundred possible thalers on one side and of a hundred actual thalers on the other, there is a difference. On this other side there are exactly a hundred thalers more. And in most real cases it is just on the hundred actual thalers that the question turns.

But the matter has a deeper aspect. One can ask the question: What is the point in the difference between a hundred possible and a hundred actual thalers? I think it would be generally conceded that for anyone who can acquire the hundred thalers, there is beyond doubt a decided difference between a hundred possible thalers and a hundred actual ones. For imagine that you are in need of a hundred thalers, and somebody lets you choose whether he is to give you the hundred possible or the hundred actual thalers. If you can get the thalers, the whole point is the difference between the two kinds. But suppose you were so placed that you cannot in any way acquire the hundred thalers, then you might feel absolutely indifferent as to whether someone did *not* give you a hundred possible or a hundred actual thalers. When a person cannot have them, then a hundred actual and a hundred possible thalers are in fact of exactly the same value.

This is a significant point. And the significance is this—that the way in which Kant spoke about God could occur only at a time when men could no longer "have God" through human soul-experience. As He could not be reached as an actuality, then the concept of the possible God or of the actual God was immaterial, just as it is immaterial whether one is *not* to have a hundred actual or a hundred possible thalers. If there is no path for the soul to the true. God, then certainly no development of thought in the style of Kant can lead to Him.

Hence we see that the matter has this deeper side also. But I have introduced it only because I wanted to make it clear that when the question becomes one of "thinking", then one must go somewhat more deeply. Errors of thought slip out even among the most brilliant thinkers, and for a long time one does not see where the weak spot of the argument lies—as, for example, in the Kantian thought about the hundred possible and the hundred actual thalers. In thinking, one must always take account of the situation in which the thought has to be grasped.

By discussing first the nature of general concepts, and then the existence of such errors in thinking as this Kantian one, I have tried to show you that one cannot properly reflect on ways of thinking without going deeply into actualities. I will now approach the matter from yet another side, a third side.

Let us suppose that we have here a mountain or hill, and beside it, a steep slope. On the slope there is a spring and the flow from it leaps sheer down, a real waterfall. Higher up on the same slope is another spring; the water from it would like to leap down in the same way, but it does not. It cannot behave as a waterfall, but runs down nicely as a stream or beck. Is the water itself endowed with different forces in these two cases? Quite clearly not. For the second stream would behave just as the first stream does if it were not obstructed by the shape of the mountain. If the obstructive force of the mountain were not present, the second stream would go leaping down. Thus we have to reckon with two forces: the obstructive force of the mountain and the earth's gravitational pull, which turns the first stream into a waterfall. The gravitational force acts also on the second stream—one can see how it brings the stream flowing down. But a sceptic could say that in the case of the second stream this is not at all obvious, whereas in the first stream every particle of water goes hurtling down. In the case of the second stream we must reckon in at every point the obstructing force of the mountain, which acts in opposition to the earth's gravitational pull.

Now suppose someone came along and said: "I don't altogether believe what you tell me about the force of gravity, nor do I believe in the obstructing force. Is the mountain the cause of the stream taking a particular path? I don't believe it." "Well, what do you believe?" one might ask. He replies: "I believe that part of the water is down there, above it is more water, above that more water again, and so on. I believe the lower water is pushed down by the water above it, and this water by the water above it. Each part of the water drives down the water below it." Here is a noteworthy distinction. The first man declares: "Gravity pulls the water down." The second man says: "Masses of water are perpetually pushing down the water below them; that is how the water comes down from above."

Obviously anyone who spoke of a "pushing down" of this kind would be very silly. But suppose it is a question not of a beck or stream but of the history of mankind, and suppose someone like the person I have just described were to say: "The only thing I believe of what you tell me is this: we are now living in the twentieth century, and during it certain events have taken place. They were brought about by similar ones during the last third of the nineteenth century; these again were caused by events in the second third of the nineteenth century, and these again by those in the first third." That is what is called "pragmatic history", in which one always speaks of "causes and effects", so that subsequent events are always explained by means of preceding ones. Just as someone might deny the force of gravity and say that the masses of water are continually pushing one another forward, so it is when someone is pursuing pragmatic history and explains the condition of the nineteenth century as a result of the French Revolution.

In reply to a pragnatic historian we would of course say: "No, other forces are active besides those that push from behind— which in fact are not there at all in the true sense. For just as little as there are forces pushing the stream from behind, just as little do preceding events push from behind in the history of humanity. Fresh influences are always coming out of the spiritual world— just as in the stream the force of gravity is always at work—and these influences cross with other forces, just as the force of gravity crosses with the obstructive force of the mountain. If only one force were present, you would see the course of history running quite differently. But you do not see the individual forces at work in history. You see only the physical ordering of the world: what we would call the results of the Saturn, Moon and Sun stages in the volution of the Earth. You do not see all that goes on continually in human souls, as they live through the spiritual world and then come down again to Earth. All this you simply deny."

But there is to-day a conception of history which is just what we would expect from somebody who came along with ideas such as those I have described, and it is by no means rare. Indeed in the nineteenth century it was looked upon as immensely clever. But what should we be able to say about it from the standpoint we have gained? If anyone were to explain the mountain stream in this "pragmatic" way, he would be talking utter nonsense. How is it then that he upholds the same nonsense with regard to history? The reason is simply that he does not notice it! And history is so complicated that it is almost everywhere expounded as "pragmatic history", and nobody notices it.

We can certainly see from this that Spiritual Science, which has to develop sound principles for the understanding of life, has work to do in the most varied domains of life; and that it is first of all necessary to learn how to think, and to get to know the inner laws and impulses of thought. Otherwise all sorts of grotesque things can befall one. Thus for example a certain man to-day is stumbling and bumbling over the problem of "thought and language". He is the celebrated language-critic Fritz Mauthner, who has also written lately a large philosophical dictionary. His bulky *Critique of Language* is already in its third edition, so for our contemporaries it is a celebrated work. There are plenty of ingenious things in this book, and plenty of dreadful ones. Thus one can find here a curious example of faulty thinking—and one runs up against such blunders in almost every five lines—which leads the worthy Mauthner to throw doubt on the need for logic. "Thinking", for him, is merely speaking; hence there is no sense in studying logic; grammar is all one needs. He says also that since there is, rightly speaking, no logic, logicians are fools. And then he says: In ordinary life, opinions are the result of inferences, and ideas come from opinions. That is how people go on! Why should there be any need for logic when we are told that opinions arise from inferences, and ideas from opinions? It is just as clever as if someone were to say: "Why do you need botany? Last year and two years ago the plants were growing." But such is the logic one finds in a man who prohibits logic. On can quite understand that he does prohibit it. There are many more remarkable things in this strange book—a book that, in regard to the relation between thought and language, leads not to lucidity but to confusion.

I said that we need a substructure for the things that are to lead us to the heights of spiritual contemplation. Such a substructure as has been put forward here may appear to many as somewhat abstract; still, we shall need it. And I think I have tried to make it so easy that what I have said is clear enough. I should like particularly to emphasise that through such simple considerations as these one can get an idea of where the boundary lies between the realm of the Spirits of Form and the realm of the Spirits of Movement. But whether one comes to such an idea is intimately connected with whether one is prepared to admit thoughts of things-in-general, or whether one is prepared to admit only ideas or concepts of individual things—I say expressly "is prepared to admit".

On these expositions—to which, as they are somewhat abstract, I will add nothing further—we will build further in the next lecture.

LECTURE TWO

THE STUDY of Spiritual Science should always go hand in hand with practical experience of how the mind works. It is impossible to get entirely clear about many things that we discussed in the last lecture unless one tries to get a kind of living grasp of what thinking involves in terms of actualities. For why is it that among the very persons whose profession it is to think about such questions, confusion reigns, for example, as to the relation between the general concept of the "triangle-in-general" and specific concepts of individual triangles? How is it that people puzzle for centuries over questions such as that of the hundred possible and the hundred real thalers cited by Kant? Why is it that people fail to pursue the very simple reflections that are necessary to see that there cannot really be any such thing as a "pragmatic" account of history, according to which the course of events always follows directly from preceding events? Why do people not reflect in such a way that they would be repelled by this impossible mode of regarding the history of man, so widely current nowadays? What is the cause of all these things?

The reason is that far too little trouble is taken over learning to handle with precision the activities of thinking, even by people whose business this should be. Nowadays everyone wants to feel that he has a perfect claim to say: "Think? Well, one can obviously do that." So they begin to think. Thus we have various conceptions of the world; there have been many philosophers—a great many. We find that one philosopher is after this and another is after that, and that many fairly clever people have drawn attention to many things. If someone comes upon contradictions in these findings, he does not ponder over them, but he is quite pleased with himself, fancying that now he can "think" indeed. He can think again what those other fellows have thought out, and feels

23

quite sure that he will find the right answer himself. For no one nowadays must make any concession to authority! That would deny the dignity of human nature! Everyone must think for himself. That is the prevailing notion in the realm of thought.

I do not know if people have reflected that this is not their attitude in other realms of life. No one feels committed to belief in authority or to a craving for authority when he has his coat made at the tailor's or his shoes at the shoemaker's. He does not say: "It would be beneath the dignity of man to let one's things be made by persons who are known to be thoroughly acquainted with their business." He may perhaps even allow that it is necessary to learn these skills. But in practical life, with regard to thinking, it is not agreed that one must get one's conceptions of the world from quarters where thinking and much else has been learnt. Only rarely would this be conceded to-day.

This is one tendency that dominates our life in the widest circles, and is the immediate reason why human thinking is not a very widespread product nowadays. I believe this can be quite easily grasped. For let us suppose that one day everybody were to say: "What!—learn to make boots? For a long time that has been unworthy of man; we can all make boots." I don't know if only good boots would come from it. At all events, with regard to the coining of correct thoughts in their conception of the world, it is from this sort of reasoning that men mostly take their start at the present day. This is what gives its deeper meaning to my remark of yesterday—that although thought is something a man is completely within, so that he can contemplate it in its inner being, actual thinking is not as common as one might suppose. Besides this, there is to-day a quite special pretension which could gradually go so far as to throw a veil over all clear thinking. We must pay attention to this also; at least we must glance at it.

Let us suppose the following. There was once in Görlitz a shoemaker named Jacob Boehme. He had learnt his craft well—how soles are cut, how the shoe is formed over the last, and how the nails are driven into the soles and leather. He knew all this down to the ground. Now supposing that this shoemaker, by name Jacob Boehme, had gone around and said: "I will now see

24

how the world is constructed. I will suppose that there is a great last at the foundation of the world. Over this last the world-leather was once stretched; then the world-nails were added, and by means of them the world-sole was fastened to the world-upper. Then boot-blacking was brought into play, and the whole world-shoe was polished. In this way I can quite clearly explain to myself how in the morning it is bright, for then the shoe-polish of the world is shining, but in the evening it is soiled with all sorts of things; it shines no longer. Hence I imagine that every night someone has the duty of repolishing the world-boot. And thus arises the difference between day and night." Let us suppose that Jacob Boehme had said this.

Yes, you laugh, for of course Jacob Boehme did not say this; but still he made good shoes for the people of Görlitz, and for that he employed his knowledge of shoe-making. But he also developed his grand thoughts, through which he wanted to build up a conception of the world; and for that he resorted to something else. He said to himself: My shoe-making is not enough for that; I dare not apply to the structure of the world the thoughts I put into making shoes. And in due course he arrived at his sublime thoughts about the world. Thus there was no such Jacob Boehme as the hypothetical figure I first sketched, but there was another one who knew how to set about things. But the hypothetical "Jacob Boehmes", like the one you laughed over—they exist everywhere to-day.

For example, we find among them physicists and chemists who have learnt the laws governing the combination and separation of substances; there are zoologists who have learnt how one examines and describes animals; there are doctors who have learnt how to treat the physical human body, and what they themselves call the soul. What do they all do? They say: When a person wants to work out for himself a conception of the world, then he takes the laws that are learnt in chemistry, in physics, or in physiology—no others are admissible—and out of these he builds a conception of the world for himself. These people proceed exactly as the hypothetical shoemaker would have done if he had constructed the world-boot, only they do not notice that their

25

world-conceptions come into existence by the very same method that produced the hypothetical world-boot. It does certainly seem rather grotesque if one imagines that the difference between day and night comes about through the soiling of shoe-leather and the repolishing of it in the night. But in terms of true logic it is in principle just the same if an attempt is made to build a world out of the laws of chemistry, physics, biology and physiology. Exactly the same principle! It is an immense presumption on the part of the physicist, the chemist, the physiologist, or the biologist, who do not wish to be anything else than physicist, chemist, physiologist, biologist, and yet want to have an opinion about the whole world. The point is that one should go to the root of things and not shirk the task of illuminating anything that is not so clear by tracing it back to its true place in the scheme of things. If you look at all this with method and logic, you will not need to be astonished that so many present-day conceptions of the world yield nothing but the "world-boot". And this is something that can point us to the study of Spiritual Science and to the pursuit of practical trains of thought; something that can urge us to examine the question of how we must think in order to see where shortcomings exist in the world.

There is something else I should like to mention in order to show where lies the root of countless misunderstandings with regard to the ideas people have about the world. When one concerns oneself with world-conceptions, does one not have over and over again the experience that someone thinks this and someone else that; one man upholds a certain view with many good reasons (one can find good reasons for everything), while another has equally good reasons for *his* view; the first man contradicts his opponent with just as good reasons as those with which the opponent contradicts him. Sects arise in the world not, in the first place, because one person or another is convinced about the right path by what is taught here or there. Only look at the paths which the disciples of great men have had to follow in order to come to this or that great man, and then you will see that herein lies something important for us with regard to karma. But if we examine the outlooks that exist in the world to-day, we must say that whether someone is a follower of Bergson, or of Haeckel, or of this or that (karma, as I have already said, does not recognise the current world-conception) depends on other things than on deep conviction. There is contention on all sides!

Yesterday I said that once there were Nominalists, persons who maintained that general concepts had no reality, but were merely names. These Nominalists had opponents who were called Realists (the word had a different meaning then). The Realists maintained that general concepts are not mere words, but refer to quite definite realities. In the Middle Ages the question of Realism versus Nominalism was always a burning one, especially for theology, a sphere of thought with which present-day thinkers trouble themselves very little. For in the time when the question of Nominalism versus Realism arose (from the eleventh to the thirteenth centuries) there was something that belonged to the most important confessions of faith, the question about the three "Divine Persons"—Father, Son and Holy Ghost—who form One Divine Being, but are still Three real Persons. The Nominalists maintained that these three Divine Persons existed only individually, the "Father" for Himself, the "Son" for Himself, and the "Holy Ghost" for Himself; and if one spoke of a "Collective God" Who comprised these Three, that was only a name for the Three. Thus Nominalism did away with the unity of the Trinity. In opposition to the Realists, the Nominalists not only explained away the unity, but even regarded it as heretical to declare, as the Realists did, that the Three Persons formed not merely an imaginary unity, but an actual one.

Thus Nominalism and Realism were opposites. And anyone who goes deeply into the literature of Realism and Nominalism during these centuries gets a deep insight into what human acumen can produce. For the most ingenious grounds were brought forward for Nominalism, just as much as for Realism. In those days it was more difficult to be reckoned as a thinker because there was no printing press, and it was not an easy thing to take part in such controversies as that between Nominalism and Realism. Anyone who ventured into this field had to be better prepared, according to the ideas of those times, than is required of people who engage in controversies nowadays. An immense amount of penetration was necessary in order to plead the cause of Realism, and it was equally so with Nominalism. How does this come about? It is grievous that things are so, and if one reflects more deeply on it, one is led to say: What use is it that you are so clever? You can be clever and plead the cause of Nominalism, and you can be just as clever and contradict Nominalism. One can get quite confused about the whole question of intelligence! It is distressing even to listen to what such characterisations are supposed to mean.

Now, as a contrast to what we have been saying, we will bring forward something that is perhaps not nearly so discerning as much that has been advanced with regard to Nominalism or to Realism, but it has perhaps one merit—it goes straight to the point and indicates the direction in which one needs to think.

Let us imagine the way in which one forms general concepts; the way in which one synthetises a mass of details. We can do this in two ways: first as a man does in the course of his life through the world. He sees numerous examples of a certain kind of animal: they are silky or woolly, are of various colours, have whiskers, at certain times they go through movements that recall human "washing", they eat mice, etc. One can call such creatures "cats". Then one has formed a general concept. All these creatures have something to do with what we call "cats". But now let us suppose that someone has had a long life, in the course of which he has encountered many cat-owners, men and women, and he has noticed that a great many of these people call their pets "Pussy". Hence he classes all these creatures under the name of "Pussy". Hence we now have the general concept "Cats" and the general concept "Pussy", and a large number of individual creatures belonging in both cases to the general concept. And yet no one will maintain that the general concept "Pussy" has the same significance as the general concept "Cats". Here the real difference comes out. In forming the general concept "Pussy" which is only a summary of names that must rank as individual names, we have taken the line, and rightly so, of Nominalism; and in forming the general concept "Cats" we have taken the line of Realism, and rightly so. In one case Nominalism is correct; in the other, Realism. Both are right. One must only apply these methods within their proper limits. And when both are right, it is not surprising that good reasons for both can be adduced. In taking the name "Pussy", I have employed a somewhat grotesque example. But I can show you a much more significant example and I will do so at once.

Within the scope of our objective experience there is a whole realm where Nominalism—the idea that the collective term is only a name—is fully justified. We have "one", "two", "three", "four", "five", and so on; but it is impossible to find in the expression "number" anything that has a real existence. "Number" has no existence. "One", "two", "three", "five", "six",— they exist. But what I said in the last lecture, that in order to find the general concept one must let that which corresponds to it pass over into movement—this cannot be done with the concept "Number". One "one" does not pass over into "two". It must always be taken as "one". Not even in thought can we pass over into two, or from two into three. Only the individual numbers exist, not "number" in general. As applied to the nature of numbers, Nominalism is entirely correct; but when we come to the single animal in relation to its genus, Realism is entirely correct. For it is impossible for a deer to exist, and another deer, and yet another, without there being the genus "deer". The figure "two" can exist for itself, "one", "seven", etc., can exist for themselves. But in so far as anything real appears in number, the number is a quality, and the concept "number" has no specific existence. External things are related to general concepts in two different ways: Nominalism is appropriate in one case, and Realism in the other.

On these lines, if we simply give our thoughts the right direction, we begin to understand why there are so many disputes about conceptions of the world. People generally are not inclined, when they have grasped one standpoint, to grasp another as well. When in some realm of thought somebody has got hold of the idea "general concepts have no existence", he proceeds to extend to it the whole make-up of the world. This sentence, "general concepts have no existence" is not false, for when applied to the particular realm which the person in question has considered, it is correct. It is only the universalising of it that is wrong. Thus it is essential, if one wants to form a correct idea of what thinking is, to understand clearly that the truth of a thought in the realm to which it belongs is no evidence for its general validity. Someone can offer me a perfectly correct proof of this or that and yet it will not hold good in a sphere to which it does not belong. Anyone, therefore, who intends to occupy himself seriously with the paths that lead to a conception of the world must recognise that the first essential is to avoid one-sidedness. That is what I specially want to bring out to-day. Now let us take a general look at some matters which will be explained in detail later on.

There are people so constituted that it is not possible for them to find the way to the Spirit, and to give them any proof of the Spirit will always be hard. They stick to something they know about, in accordance with their nature. Let us say they stick at something that makes the crudest kind of impression on them— *Materialism*. We need not regard as foolish the arguments they advance as a defence or proof of Materialism, for an immense amount of ingenious writing has been devoted to the subject, and it holds good in the first place for material life, for the material world and its laws.

Again, there are people who, owing to a certain inwardness, are naturally predisposed to see in all that is material only the revelation of the spiritual. Naturally, they know as well as the materialists do that, externally, the material world exists; but matter, they say, is only the revelation, the manifestation, of the underlying spiritual. Such persons may take no particular interest in the material world and its laws. As all their ideas of the spiritual come to them through their own inner activity, they may go through the world with the consciousness that the true, the lofty, in which one ought to interest oneself—all genuine reality—is found only in the the Spirit; that matter is only illusion, only external phantasmagoria. This would be an extreme standpoint, but it can occur, and can lead to a complete denial of material life. We should have to say of such persons that they certainly do recognise what is most real, the Spirit, but they are one-sided; they deny the significance of the material world and its laws. Much acute thinking can be enlisted in support of the conception of the universe held by these persons. Let us call their conception of the universe, *Spiritism*. Can we say that the Spiritists are right? As regards the Spirit, their contentions could bring to light some exceptionally correct ideas, but concerning matter and its laws they might reveal very little of any significance. Can one say that the Materialists are correct in what they maintain? Yes, concerning matter and its laws they may be able to discover some exceptionally useful and valuable facts; but in speaking of the Spirit they may utter nothing but foolishness. Hence we must say that both parties are correct in their respective spheres.

There can also be persons who say: "Yes, but as to whether in truth the world contains only matter, or only spirit, I have no special knowledge; the powers of human cognition cannot cope with that. One thing is clear—there is a world spread out around us. Whether it is based upon what chemists and physicists, if they are materialists, call atoms, I know not. But I recognise the external world; that is something I see and can think about. I have no particular reason for supposing that it is or is not spiritual at root. I restrict myself to what I see around me." From the explanations already given we can call such persons Realists, and their concept of the universe, *Realism*. Just as one can enlist endless ingenuity on behalf of Materialism or of Spiritism, and just as one can be clever about Spiritism and yet say the most foolish things on material matters, and vice versa, so one can advance the most ingenious reasons for Realism, which differs from both Spiritism and Materialism in the way I have just described.

Again, there may be other persons who speak as follows. Around us are matter and the world of material phenomena. But this world of material phenomena is in itself devoid of meaning. It has no real meaning unless there is within it a progressive tendency; unless from this external world something can emerge towards which the human soul can direct itself, independently of the world. According to this outlook, there must be a realm of ideas and ideals within the world-process. Such people are not

Realists, although they pay external life its due; their view is that life has meaning only if ideas work through it and give it purpose. It was under the influence of such a mood as this that Fichte once said: Our world is the sensualised material of our duty.* The adherents of such a world-outlook as this, which takes everything as a vehicle for the ideas that permeate the world-process, may be called Idealists and their outlook, *Idealism*. Beautiful and grand and glorious things have been brought forward on behalf of this Idealism. And in this realm that I have just described—where the point is to show that the world would be purposeless and meaningless if ideas were only human inventions and were not rooted in the world-process—in this realm Idealism is fully justified. But by means of it one cannot, for example, explain external reality. Hence one can distinguish this Idealism from other world-outlooks:

Materialism

Idealism   Realism

Spiritism

We now have side by side four justifiable world-outlooks, each with significance for its particular domain. Between Materialism and Idealism there is a certain transition. The crudest kind of materialism—one can observe it specially well in our day, although it is already on the wane—will consist in this, that people carry to an extreme the saying of Kant—Kant did not do this himself!—that in the individual sciences there is only so much real science as there is mathematics. This means that from being a materialist one can become a ready-reckoner of the universe, taking nothing as valid except a world composed of material atoms. They collide and gyrate, and then one calculates how they inter-gyrate. By this means one obtains very fine results, which

---

* "*Unsere Welt ist das versinnlichte Material unserer Pflicht.*" The rendering given is that of Professor Robert Adamson, in the series of Blackwood's Philosophical Classics for English readers. Alternative words for *versinnlichte* might be "sense-perceptible" or "tangible". The quotation is from Fichte's work, *Über den Grund unseres Glaubens an eine göttliche Weltregierung* (1798).

show that this way of looking at things is fully justified. Thus you can get the vibration-rates for blue, red, etc.; you take the whole world as a kind of mechanical apparatus, and can reckon it up accurately. But one can become rather confused in this field. One can say to oneself: "Yes, but however complicated the machine may be, one can never get out of it anything like the perception of blue, red, etc. Thus if the brain is only a complicated machine, it can never give rise to what we know as soul-experiences." But then one can say, as Du Bois-Raymond once said: If we want to explain the world in strictly mathematical terms, we shall not be able to explain the simplest perception, but if we go outside a mathematical explanation, we shall be unscientific. The most uncompromising materialist would say, "No, I do not even calculate, for that would presuppose a superstition—it would imply that I assume that things are ordered by measure and number." And anyone who raises himself above this crude materialism will become a mathematical thinker, and will recognise as valid only whatever can be treated mathematically. From this results a conception of the universe that really admits nothing beyond mathematical formulae. This may be called *Mathematism*.

Someone, however, might think this over, and after becoming a Mathematist he might say to himself: "It cannot be a super-stition that the colour blue has so and so many vibrations. The world is ordered mathematically. If mathematical ideas are found to be real in the world, why should not other ideas have equal reality?" Such a person accepts this—that ideas are active in the world. But he grants validity only to those ideas that he discovers outside himself—not to any ideas that he might grasp from his inner self by some sort of intuition or inspiration, but only to those he reads from external things that are real to the senses. Such a person becomes a Rationalist, and his outlook on the world is that of *Rationalism*. If, in addition to the ideas that are found in this way, someone grants validity also to those gained from the moral and the intellectual realms, then he is already an Idealist. Thus a path leads from crude Materialism, by way of Mathematism and Rationalism, to Idealism.

33

But now Idealism can be enhanced. In our age there are some men who are trying to do this. They find ideas at work in the world, and this implies that there must also be in the world some sort of beings in whom the ideas can live. Ideas cannot live just as they are in any external object, nor can they hang as it were in the air. In the nineteenth century the belief existed that ideas rule history. But this was a confusion, for ideas as such have no power to work. Hence one cannot speak of ideas in history. Anyone who understands that ideas, if they are there are all, are bound up with some *being* capable of having ideas, will no longer be a mere Idealist; he will move on to the supposition that ideas are connected with beings. He becomes a Psychist and his world-outlook is that of *Psychism*. The Psychist, who in his turn can uphold his outlook with an immense amount of ingenuity, reaches it only through a kind of one-sidedness, of which he can eventually become aware.

Materialism

Mathematism

Rationalism

Idealism ←————————————→ Realism

Psychism

Spiritism

Here I must add that there are adherents of all the world-outlooks above the horizontal stroke; for the most part they are stubborn folk who, owing to some fundamental element in themselves, take this or that world-outlook and abide by it, going no further. All the beliefs listed below the line have adherents who are more easily accessible to the knowledge that individual world-outlooks each have one special standpoint only, and they more easily reach the point where they pass from one world-outlook to another.

When someone is a Psychist, and able as a thinking person to contemplate the world clearly, then he comes to the point of saying to himself that he must presuppose something actively psychic in the outside world. But directly he not only thinks, but feels sympathy for what is active and willing in man, then he says to himself: "It is not enough that there are beings who have ideas; these beings must also be active, they must be able also to do things." But this is inconceivable unless these beings are individual beings. That is, a person of this type rises from accepting the ensoulment of the world to accepting the Spirit or the Spirits of the world. He is not yet clear whether he should accept one or a number of Spirits, but he advances from Psychism to *Pneumatism*, to a doctrine of the Spirit.

Materialism

Mathematism

Rationalism

Idealism ←——————————————→ Realism

Psychism

Pneumatism

Spiritism

If he has become in truth a Pneumatist, then he may well grasp what I have said in this lecture about number—that with regard to figures it is somewhat doubtful to speak of a "unity". Then he comes to the point of saying to himself: It must therefore be a confusion to talk of one undivided Spirit, of one undivided Pneuma. And he gradually becomes able to form for himself an idea of the Spirits of the different Hierarchies. Then he becomes in the true sense a Spiritist, so that on this side there is a direct transition from Pneumatism to Spiritism.

These world-outlooks are all justified in their own fields. For there are fields where Psychism acts illuminatingly, and others where Pneumatism does the same. Certainly, anyone who wishes to deliberate about an explanation of the universe as thoroughly as we have tried to do must come to Spiritism, to the acceptance of the Spirits of the Hierarchies. For to stop short at Pneumatism would in this case mean the following. If we are Spiritists, then it may happen that people will say to us: "Why so many spirits? Why bring numbers into it? Let there be One Undivided Spirit!" Anyone who goes more deeply into the matter knows that this objection is like saying: "You tell me there are two hundred midges over there. I don't see two hundred; I see only a single swarm." Exactly so would an adherent of Pneumatism stand with regard to a Spiritist. The Spiritist sees the universe filled with the Spirits of the Hierarchies; the Pneumatist sees only the one "swarm"—only the Universal Spirit. But that comes from an inexact view.

Now there is still another possibility: someone may not take the path we have tried to follow to the activities of the spiritual Hierarchies, but may still come to an acceptance of certain spiritual beings. The celebrated German philosopher, Leibnitz, was a man of this kind. Leibnitz had got beyond the prejudice that anything merely material can exist in the world. He found the actual, he sought the actual. (I have treated this more precisely in my book, *The Riddles of Philosophy*.) His view was that a being —as, for example, the human soul—can build up existence in itself. But he formed no further ideas on the subject. He only said to himself that there is such a being that can build up existence in itself, and force concepts outwards from within itself. For Leibnitz, this being is a "Monad". And he said to himself: "There must be many Monads, and Monads of the most varied capabilities. If I had here a bell, there would be many monads in it— as in a swarm of midges—but they would be monads that had never come even so far as to have sleep-consciousness, monads that are almost unconscious, but which nevertheless develop the dimmest of concepts within themselves. There are monads that dream; there are monads that develop waking ideas within themselves; in short, there are monads of the most varied grades."

A person with this outlook does not come so far as to picture to himself the individual spiritual beings in concrete terms, as the Spiritist does, but he reflects in the world upon the spiritual element in the world, allowing it to remain indefinite. He calls it "Monad"—that is, he conceives of it only as though one were to say: "Yes, there is spirit in the world and there are spirits, but I describe them only by saying, 'They are entities having varying powers of perception.' I pick out from them an abstract characteristic. So I form for myself this one-sided world-outlook, on behalf of which as much as can be said as has been said by the highly intelligent Leibnitz. In this way I develop Monadism." *Monadism* is an abstract Spiritism.

But there can be persons who do not rise to the level of the Monads; they cannot concede that existence is made up of being with the most varied conceptual powers, but at the same time they are not content to allow reality only to external phenomena; they hold that "forces" are dominant everywhere. If, for example, a stone falls to the ground, they say, "That is gravitation!" When a magnet attracts bits of iron, they say: "That is magnetic force!" They are not content with saying simply, "There is the magnet," but they say, "The magnet presupposes that supersensibly, invisibly, a magnetic force is present, extending in all directions." A world-outlook of this kind—which looks everywhere for forces behind phenomena, can be called *Dynamism*.

Materialism

Mathematism

Rationalism

Idealism ⟵——————————⟶ Realism

Psychism   Dynamism

Pneumatism   Monadism

Spiritism

Then one may say: "No, to believe in 'forces' is superstition" —an example of this is Fritz Mauthner's *Critique of Language*, where you find a detailed argument to this effect. It amounts to taking your stand on the reality of the things around us. Thus by the path of Spiritism we come through Monadism and Dynamism to Realism again.

But now one can do something else still. One can say: "Certainly I believe in the world that is spread out around me, but I do not maintain any right to claim that this world is the real one. I can say of it only that it 'appears' to me. I have no right to say more about it." There you have again a difference. One can say of the world that is spread out around us, "This is the real world," but one can also say, "I am clear that there is a world which appears to me; I cannot speak of anything more. I am not saying that this world of colours and sounds, which arises only because certain processes in my eyes present themselves to me as colours, while processes in my ears present themselves to me as sounds—I am not saying that this world is the true world. It is a world of phenomena." This is the outlook called *Phenomenalism*.

We can go further, and can say: "The world of phenomena we certainly have around us, but all that we believe we have in these phenomena is what we have ourselves added to them, what we have thought into them. Our own sense-impressions are all we can rightly accept. Anyone who says this—mark it well!—is not an adherent of Phenomenalism. He peels off from the phenomena everything which he thinks comes only from the understanding and the reason, and he allows validity only to sense-impressions, regarding them as some kind of message from reality. This outlook may be called *Sensationalism*.

A critic of this outlook can then say: "You may reflect as much as you like on what the senses tell us and bring forward ever so ingenious reasons for your view—and ingenious reasons can be given—I take my stand on the point that nothing real exists except that which manifests itself through sense-impressions; this I accept as something material." This is rather like an atomist saying: "I hold that only atoms exist, and that however small they are, they have the attributes which we recognise in the physical world"—anyone who says this is a materialist. Thus, by another path, we arrive back at Materialism.

Materialism

Mathematism   Sensationalism

Rationalism   Phenomenalism

Idealism ←————————————————→ Realism

Psychism   Dynamism

Pneumatism   Monadism

Spiritism

All these conceptions of the world that I have described and written down for you really exist, and they can be maintained. And it is possible to bring forward the most ingenious reasons for each of them; it is possible to adopt any one of them and with ingenious reasons to refute the others. In between these conceptions of the world one can think out yet others, but they differ only in degree from the leading types I have described, and can be traced back to them. If one wishes to learn about the web and woof of the world, then one must know that the way to it is through these twelve points of entry. There is not merely one conception of the world that can be defended, or justified, but there are twelve. And one must admit that just as many good reasons can be adduced for each and all of them as for any particular one. The world cannot be rightly considered from the one-sided standpoint of one single conception, one single mode of thought; the world discloses itself only to someone who knows that one must look at it from all sides. Just as the sun—if we go by the Copernican conception of the universe—passes through the signs of the Zodiac in order to illuminate the earth from

39

twelve different points, so we must not adopt one standpoint, the standpoint of Idealism, or Sensationalism, or Phenomenalism, or any other conception of the world with a name of this kind; we must be in a position to go all round the world and accustom ourselves to the twelve different standpoints from which it can be contemplated. In terms of thought, all twelve standpoints are fully justifiable. For a thinker who can penetrate into the nature of thought, there is not one single conception of the world, but twelve that can be equally justified—so far justified as to permit of equally good reasons being thought out for each of them. There are twelve such justified conceptions of the world.

Tomorrow we will start from the points of view we have gained in this way, so that from the consideration of man in terms of thought we may rise to a consideration of the cosmic.

LECTURE THREE

YESTERDAY I TRIED to set forth those world-outlooks which are possible for man; so possible that certain valid proofs can be produced for the correctness of each of them in a certain realm. For anyone who is not concerned to weld together into a single system all that he has been in a position to observe and reflect upon in a certain limited domain, and then sets out to seek proofs for it, but who wants to penetrate into the truth of the world, it is important to realise that broadmindedness is necessary because twelve typical varieties of world-outlook are actually possible for the mind of man. (For the moment we need not go into the transitional ones.) If one wants to come really to the truth, then one must try clearly to understand the significance of these twelve typical varieties, must endeavour to recognise for what domain of existence one or other variety holds the best key. If we let these twelve varieties pass once again before our mind's eye, as we did yesterday, then we find that they are: Materialism, Sensationalism, Phenomenalism, Realism, Dynamism, Monadism, Spiritism, Pneumatism, Psychism, Idealism, Rationalism and Mathematism.

Now in the actual field of human searching after truth it is unfortunate that individual minds, individual personalities, always incline to let one or the other of these varieties have the upper hand, with the result that different epochs develop one-sided outlooks which then work back on the people living at that time.

We had better arrange the twelve world-outlooks in the form of a circle (see page 50), and quietly observe them. They are possible, and one must know them. They really stand in such a relation to one another that they form a mental copy of the Zodiac with which we are now so well acquainted. As the sun apparently passes through the Zodiac, and as other planets apparently do the same, so it is possible for the human soul to pass through a mental circle which embraces twelve world-pictures. Indeed, one can even bring the characteristics of these pictures into connection with the individual signs of the Zodiac, and this is in no wise arbitrary, for between the individual signs of the Zodiac and the Earth there really is a connection similar to that between the twelve world-outlooks and the human soul. I mean this in the following sense.

We could not say that there is an easily understandable relation between, e.g. the sign Aries and the Earth. But when the Sun, Saturn, or Mercury are so placed that from the Earth they are seen in the sign Aries, then influence is different from what it is when they are seen in the sign Leo. Thus the effect which comes to us out of the Cosmos from the different planets varies according as the individual planets stand in one or other of the Zodiacal signs. In the case of the human soul, it is even easier to recognise the effects of these twelve "mental-zodiacal-signs" (*Geistes-Tierkreisbilder*). There are souls who have the tendency to receive a given influence on their inner life, on their scientific, philosophic or other mental proclivities, so that their souls are open to be illuminated, as it were, by Idealism. Other souls are open to be shone upon by Materialism, others by Sensationalism. A man is not a Sensationalist, Materialist, Spiritist or Pneumatist because this or that world-outlook is—and can be seen to be—correct, but because his soul is so conditioned that it is predominantly influenced by the respective mental-zodiacal-sign. Thus in the twelve mental-zodiacal-signs we have something that can lead us to a deep insight into the way in which human world-outlooks arise, and can help us to see far into the reasons why, on the one hand, men dispute about world-outlooks, and why, on the other hand, they ought not to dispute but would do much better to understand why it happens that people have different world-outlooks. How, in spite of this, it may be necessary for certain epochs strongly to oppose the trend of this or the other world-outlook, we shall have to explain in the next lecture. What I have said so far refers to the moulding of human thought by the spiritual cosmos of the twelve zodiacal signs, which form as it were our spiritual horizon.

But there is still something else that determines human world-outlooks. You will best understand this if I first of all show you the following.

A man can be so attuned in his soul—for the present it is immaterial by which of these twelve "mental-zodiacal-signs" his soul is illuminated—that the soul-mood expressed in the whole configuration of his world-outlook can be designated as Gnosis. A man is a Gnostic when his disposition is such that he gets to know the things of the world not through the senses, but through certain cognitional forces in the soul itself. A man can be a Gnostic and at the same time have a certain inclination to be illuminated by e.g. the mental-zodiacal-sign that we have here called "Spiritism". Then his Gnosticism will have a deeply illuminated insight into the relationships of the spiritual worlds. But a man can also be, e.g. a Gnostic of Idealism; then he will have a special proclivity for seeing clearly the ideals of mankind and the ideas of the world. Thus there can be a difference between two men who are both Idealists. One man will be an idealistic enthusiast who always has the word "ideal", "ideal", "ideal", on his lips, but does not know much about idealism; he lacks the faculty for conjuring up ideals in sharp outline before his inner sight. The other man not only speaks of Idealism, but knows how to picture the ideals clearly in his soul. The latter, who inwardly grasps Idealism quite concretely—as intensely as a man grasps external things with his hand—is a Gnostic in the domain of Idealism. Thus one could say that he is basically a Gnostic, but is specially illuminated by the mental-zodiacal-sign of Idealism.

There are also persons who are specially illuminated by the world-outlook sign of Realism. They go through the world in such a way that their whole mode of perceiving and encountering the world enables them to say much, very much, to others about the world. They are neither Spiritists nor Idealists; they are quite ordinary Realists. They are equipped to have really fine perceptions of the external reality around them, and of the intrinsic qualities of things. They are Gnostics, genuine Gnostics, only they are Gnostics of Realism. There are such Gnostics of Realism, and Spiritists or Idealists are often not Gnostics of Realism at all. We can indeed find that people who call themselves good Theosophists may go through a picture-gallery and understand nothing about it, whereas others who are not Theosophists at all, but are Gnostics of Realism, are able to make an abundance of significant comments on it, because with their whole personality they are in touch with the reality of the things they see. Or again, many Theosophists go out into the country and are unable to grasp with their whole souls anything of the greatness and sublimity of nature; they are not Gnostics of Realism.

There are also Gnostics of Materialism. Certainly they are strange Gnostics. But quite in the sense in which there are Gnostics of Realism, there can be Gnostics of Materialism. They are persons who have feeling and perception only for all that is material; persons who try to get to know what the material is by coming into direct contact with it, like the dog who sniffs at substances and tries to get to know them intimately in that way, and who really is, in regard to material things, an excellent Gnostic. One can be a Gnostic in connection with all twelve world-outlook signs. Hence, if we want to put Gnosis in its right place, we must draw a circle, and the whole circle signifies that the Gnosis can move round through all twelve world-outlook signs. Just as a planet goes through all twelve signs of the Zodiac, so can the Gnosis pass through the twelve world-outlook signs. Certainly, the Gnosis will render the greatest service for the healing of souls when the Gnostic frame of mind is applied to Spiritism. One might say that Gnosis is thoroughly at home in Spiritism. That is its true home. In the other world-outlook-signs it is outside its home. Logically speaking, one is not justified in saying that there could not be a materialistic Gnosis. The pedants of concepts and ideas can settle such knotty points more easily than the sound logicians, who have a somewhat more complicated task. One might say, for example: "I will call nothing 'Gnosis' except what penetrates into the 'spirit'." That is an arbitrary attitude with regard to concepts; as arbitrary as if one were to say: "So far I have seen violets only in Austria; therefore I call

violets only flowers that grow in Austria and have a violet colour
—nothing else." Logically it is just as impossible to say that there
is Gnosis only in the world-outlook-sign of Spiritism; for Gnosis
is a "planet" which passes through all the mental-constellations.

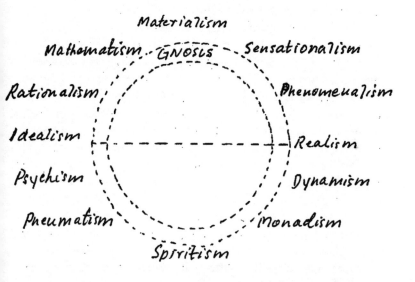

There is another world-outlook-mood. Here I speak of
"mood", whereas otherwise I speak of "signs" or "pictures". Of
late it has been thought that one could more easily become
acquainted—and yet here even the easy is difficult—with this
second mood, because its representative, in the constellation of
Idealism, is Hegel, But this special mood in which Hegel looks at
the world need not be in the constellation of Idealism, for it, too,
can pass through all the constellations. It is the world-outlook of
Logicism. The special mark of Logicism consists in its enabling the
soul to connect thoughts, concepts and ideas with one another. As
when in looking at an organism one comes from the eyes to the
nose and the mouth and regards them as all belonging to each
other, so Hegel arranges all the concepts that he can lay hold of
into a great concept-organism—a logical concept-organism. Hegel
was simply able to seek out everything in the world that can be

found as thought, to link together thought with thought, and to make an organism of it—Logicism! One can develop Logicism in the constellation of Idealism, as Hegel did; one can develop it, as Fichte did, in the constellation of Psychism; and one can develop it in other constellations. Logicism is again something that passes like a planet through the twelve zodiacal signs.

There is a third mood of the soul, expressed in world-outlooks; we can study this in Schopenhauer, for example. Whereas the soul of Hegel when he looked out upon the world was so attuned that with him everything conceptual takes the form of Logicism, Schopenhauer lays hold of everything in the soul that pertains to the character of will. The forces of nature, the hardness of a stone, have this character for him; the whole of reality is a manifestation of will. This arises from the particular disposition of his soul. This outlook can once more be regarded as a planet which passes through all twelve zodiacal signs. I will call this world-outlook, *Voluntarism*.

Schopenhauer was a voluntarist, and in his soul he was so constituted that he laid himself open to the influence of the mental constellation of Psychism. Thus arose the peculiar Schopenhauerian metaphysics of the will: Voluntarism in the mental constellation of Psychism.

Let us suppose that someone is a Voluntarist, with a special inclination towards the constellation of Monadism. Then he would not, like Schopenhauer, take as basis of the universe a unified soul which is really "will"; he would take many "monads", which are, however, will-entities. This world of monadic voluntarism has been developed most beautifully, ingeniously, and I might say, in the most inward manner, by the Austrian philosophic poet, Hamerling. Whence came the peculiar teaching that you find in Hamerling's *Atomistics of the Will*? It arose because his soul was attuned to Voluntarism, while he came under the mental constellation of Monadism. If we had the time, we could mention examples for each soul-mood in each constellation. They are to be found in the world.

Another special mood is not at all prone to ponder whether behind the phenomena there is still this or that, as is done by the gnostic mood, or by the idealistic or voluntary moods, but which simply says: "I will incorporate into my world-conception whatever I meet with in the world, whatever shows itself to me externally." One can do this in all domains—i.e. through all mental constellations. One can do it as a materialist who accepts only what he encounters externally; one can also do it as spiritist. A man who has this mood will not trouble himself to seek for a special connection behind the phenomena; he lets things approach and waits for whatever comes from them. This mood we can call *Empiricism*. Empiricism signifies a soul-mood which simply accepts whatever experience may offer. Through all twelve constellations one can be an empiricist, a man with a world-conception based on experience. Empiricism is the fourth psychic mood which can go through all twelve constellations.

One can equally well develop a mood which is not satisfied with immediate experience, as in Empiricism, so that one feels through and through, as an inner necessity, a mood which says: Man is placed in the world; in his soul he experiences something about the world that he cannot experience externally; only there, in that inner realm, does the world unveil its secrets. One may look all round about and yet see nothing of the mysteries which the world includes. Someone imbued with a mood of this kind can often say: "Of what help to me is the Gnosis that takes pains to struggle up to a kind of vision? The things of the external world that one can look upon—they cannot show me the truth. How does Logicism help me to a world-picture? . . . In Logicism the nature of the world does not express itself. What help is there in speculations about the will? It merely leads us away from looking into the depths of our own soul, and into those depths one does not look when the soul wills, but, on the contrary, just when by surrendering itself it is without will." Voluntarism, therefore, is not the mood that I mean here, neither is Empiricism—the mere looking upon and listening to experience and events. But when the soul has become quiet and seeks inwardly for the divine Light, this soul-mood can be called *Mysticism*.

Again, one can be a mystic through all the twelve mental constellations. It would certainly not be specially favourable if one were a mystic of materialism—i.e. if one experienced inwardly not the mental, the spiritual, but the material. For a mystic of materialism is really he who has acquired a specially fine perception of how one feels when one enjoys this or that substance. It is somewhat different if one imbibes the juice of this plant or the other, and then waits to see what happens to one's organism. One thus grows together with matter in one's experience; one becomes a mystic of matter. This can even become an "awakening" for life, so that one follows up how one substance or another, drawn from this or that plant, works upon the organism, affecting particularly this or that organ. And so to be a Mystic of Materialism is a precondition for investigating individual substances in respect of their healing powers.

One can be a Mystic of the world of matter, and one can be a Mystic of Idealism. An ordinary Idealist or a Gnostic Idealist is not a Mystic of Idealism. A Mystic of Idealism is one who has above all the possibility in his own soul of bringing out from its hidden sources the ideals of humanity, of feeling them as something Divine, and of placing them in that light before the soul. We have an example of the Mystic of Idealism in Meister Eckhardt.

Now the soul may be so attuned that it cannot become aware of what may arise from within itself and appear as the real inner solution of the riddle of the universe. Such a soul may, rather, be so attuned that it will say to itself: "Yes, in the world there is something behind all things, and also behind my own personality and being, so far as I perceive this being. But I cannot be a mystic. The mystic believes that this something behind flows into his soul. I do not feel it flow into my soul; I only feel it must be there, outside." In this mood, a person presupposes that outside his soul, and beyond anything his soul can experience, the essential being of things lies hidden; but he does not suppose that this essential nature of things can flow into his soul, as does the Mystic. A person who takes this standpoint is a Transcendentalist—perhaps that is the best word for it. He accepts that the essence of a thing is transcendent, but that it does not enter into the soul—hence *Transcendentalism*. The Transcendentalist has the feeling: "When

I perceive things, their nature approaches me; but I do not perceive it. It hides behind, but it approaches me."

Now it is possible for a man, given all his perceptions and powers of cognition, to thrust away the nature of things still further than the Transcendentalist does. He can say: "The essential nature of things is beyond the range of ordinary human knowledge." The Transcendentalist says: "If with your eyes you see red and blue, then the essential being of the thing is not in the red or blue, but lies hidden behind it. You must use your eyes; then you can get to the essential being of the thing. It lies behind." But the mood I now have in mind will not accept Transcendentalism. On the contrary, it says: "One may experience red or blue, or this or that sound, ever so intensely; nothing of this expresses the hidden being of the thing. My perception never makes contact with this hidden being." Anyone who speaks in this way speaks very much as we do when we take the standpoint that in external sense-appearance, in Maya, the essential nature of things does not find expression. We should be Transcendentalists if we said: "The world is spread out all around us, and this world everywhere proclaims its essential being." This we do not say. We say: "This world is Maya, and one must seek the inner being of things by another way than through external sense-perception and the ordinary means of cognition." *Occultism!* The psychic mood of Occultism!

Again, one can be an Occultist throughout all the mental-zodiacal signs. One can even be a thorough Occultist of Materialism. Yes, the rationally-minded scientists of the present day are all occultists of materialism, for they talk of "atoms". But if they are not irrational it will never occur to them to declare that with any kind of "method" one can come to the atom. The atom remains in the occult. It is only that they do not like to be called "Occultists", but they are so in the fullest sense of the word.

Apart from the seven world-outlooks I have drawn here, there can be no others—only transitions from one to another, Thus we must not only distinguish twelve various shades of world-outlook which are at rest round the circle, so to speak, but we must recognise that in each of the shades a quite special mood

49

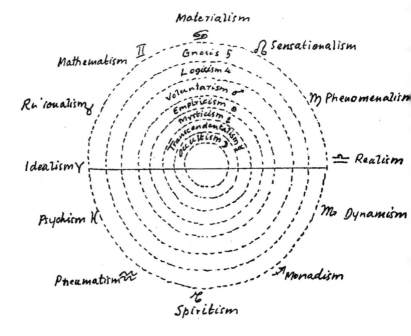

Materialism
Sensationalism
Mathematism
Gnosis 5
Logicism 4
Voluntarism 3
Empiricism 2
Mysticism 1
Transcendentalism
Occultism 7
Rationalism
Phenomenalism
Idealism
Realism
Psychism
Dynamism
Pneumatism
Monadism
Spiritism

of the human soul is possible. From this you can see how immensely varied are the outlooks open to human personalities. One can specially cultivate each of these seven world-outlook-moods, and each of them can exist in one or other shade.

What I have just depicted is actually the spiritual correlative of what we find externally in the world as the relations between the signs of the Zodiac and the planets, the seven planets familiar in Spiritual Science. Thus we have an external picture (not invented, but standing out there in the cosmos) for the relations of our seven world-outlook-moods to our twelve shades of world-outlook. We shall have the right feeling for this picture if we contemplate it in the following manner.

Let us begin with Idealism, and let us mark it with the mental-zodiacal sign of *Aries*; in like manner let us mark Rationalism as *Taurus*, Mathematism as *Gemini*, Materialism as *Cancer*, Sensationalism as *Leo*, Phenomenalism as *Virgo*, Realism as *Libra*, Dynamism as *Scorpio*, Monadism as *Sagittarius*, Spiritism as *Capricorn*, Pneumatism as *Aquarius*, and Psychism as *Pisces*. The relations which exist spatially between the individual zodiacal signs are actually present between these shades of world-outlook in the realm of spirit. And the relations which are entered into by the planets, as they follow their orbits through the Zodiac, correspond to the relations which the seven world-outlook-moods enter into, so that we can feel Gnosticism as Saturn, Logicism as Jupiter, Voluntarism as Mars, Empiricism as Sun, Mysticism as Venus, Transcendentalism as Mercury, and Occultism as Moon (see diagram, p. 50).

Even in the external pictures—although the main thing is that the innermost connections correspond—you will find something similar. The Moon remains occult, invisible when it is New Moon; it must have the light of the Sun brought to it, just as occult things remain occult until, through meditation, concentration and so on, the powers of the soul rise up and illuminate them. A person who goes through the world and relies only on the Sun, who accepts only what the Sun illuminates, is an Empiricist. A person who reflects on what the Sun illuminates, and retains the thoughts after the Sun has set, is no longer an Empiricist, because he no longer depends upon the Sun. "Sun" is the symbol of Empiricism. I might take all this further but we have only four periods to spend on this important subject, and for the present I must leave you to look for more exact connections, either throughout your own thinking or through other investigations. The connections are not difficult to find when the model has been given.

Broadmindedness is all too seldom sought. Anyone really in earnest about truth would have to be able to represent the twelve shades of world-outlook in his soul. He would have to know in terms of his own experience what it means to be a Gnostic, a Logician, a Voluntarist, an Empiricist, a Mystic, a Transcendentalist, an Occultist. All this must be gone through experimentally by anyone who wants to penetrate into the secrets of the universe according to the ideas of Spiritual Science. Even if what you will find in the book, *Knowledge of the Higher Worlds*, does not exactly fit in with this account, it is really depicted only from other points of view, and can lead us into the single moods which are here designated as the Gnostic mood, the Jupiter mood, and so on.

Often a man is so one-sided that he lets himself be influenced by only one constellation, by one mood. We find this particularly in great men. Thus, for example, Hamerling is an out-and-out Monadist or a monadologistic Voluntarist; Schopenhauer is a pronounced voluntaristic Psychist. It is precisely great men who have so adjusted their souls that their world-outlook-mood stands in a definite spiritual constellation. Other people get on much more easily with the different standpoints, as they are called. But it can also happen that men are stimulated from various sides in reaching their world-outlook, or for what they place before themselves as world-outlook. Thus someone may be a good Logician, but his logical mood stands in the constellation of Sensationalism; he can at the same time be a good Empiricist, but his empirical mood stands in the constellation of Mathematism. This may happen. When it does happen, a quite definite world-outlook is produced. Just at the present time we have an example of the outlook that comes about through someone having his Sun—in the spiritual sense—in Gemini, and his Jupiter in Leo; such a man is Wundt. And all the details in the philosophical writings of Wundt can be grasped when the secret of his special psychic configuration has been penetrated.

The effect is specially good when a person has experienced, by way of exercises, the various psychic moods—Occultism, Transcendentalism, Mysticism, Empiricism, Voluntarism, Logicism, Gnosis—so that he can conjure them up in his mind and feel all their effects at once, and can then place all these moods together in the constellation of Phenomenalism, in Virgo. Then there actually comes before him as phenomena, and with a quite special magnificence, that which can be unveiled for him in a remarkable way as the content of his world-picture. When, in the same way, the individual world-outlook-moods are brought one after another in relation to another constellation, then it is not so good. Hence in many ancient Mystery-schools, just this mood, with all the soul-planets standing in the spiritual constellation of Virgo, was induced in the pupils because it was through this that they

could most easily fathom the world. They grasped the phenomena, but they grasped them "gnostically". They were in a
position to pass behind the thought-phenomena, but they had no
crude experience of the will: that would happen only if the
soul-mood of Voluntarism were placed in Scorpio. In short, by
means of the constellation given through the world-outlook-
moods—the planetary element—and through the nuances connected with the spiritual Zodiac, the world-picture which a
person carries with him through a given incarnation is called forth.

But there is one more thing. These world-pictures—they have
many nuances if you reckon with all their combinations—are
modified yet again by possessing quite definite tones. But we have
only three tones to distinguish. All world-pictures, all combinations which arise in this manner, can appear in one of three ways.
First, they can be theistic, so that what appears in the soul as tone
must be called *Theism*. Or, in contrast to Theism, there may be a
soul-tone that we must call *Intuitionism*. Theism arises when a
person clings to all that is external in order to find his God, when
he seeks his God in the external. The ancient Hebrew Monotheism
was a particularly "theistic" world-outlook. Intuitionism arises
when a person seeks his world-picture especially through intuitive
flashes from his inner depths. And there is a third tone, *Naturalism*.

These three psychic tones are reflected in the cosmos, and their
relation to one another in the soul of man is exactly like that of
Sun, Moon and Earth, so that Theism corresponds to the Sun—
the Sun being here considered as a fixed star—Intuitionism to the
Moon, and Naturalism to the Earth. If we transpose the entities
here designated as Sun, Moon and Earth into the spiritual, then a
man who goes beyond the phenomena of the world and says:
"When I look around, then God, Who fills the world, reveals
Himself to me in everything," or a man who stands up when he
comes into the rays of the sun—they are Theists. A man who is
content to study the details of natural phenomena, without going
beyond them, and equally a man who pays no attention to the
sun but only to its effects on the earth—he is a Naturalist. A man
who seeks for the best, guided by his intuitions—he is like the
intuitive poet whose soul is stirred by the mild silvery glance of

the moon to sing its praises. Just as one can bring moonlight into connection with imagination, so the occultist, the Intuitionist, as we mean him here, must be brought into relation with the moon.

Lastly there is a special thing. It occurs only in a single case, when a person, taking all the world-pictures to some extent, restricts himself only to what he can experience on or around or in himself. That is *Anthropomorphism*. Such a person corresponds to the man who observes the Earth on its own account, independently of its being shone upon by the Sun, the Moon, or anything else. Just as we can consider the Earth for itself alone, so also with regard to world-outlooks we can reckon only with what as men we can find in ourselves. So does a widespread Anthropomorphism arise in the world. If one goes out beyond man in himself, as one must go out to Sun and Moon for an explanation of the phenomenon of the Earth—something that present-day science does not do—then one comes to recognise three different things, Theism, Intuitionism and Naturalism side by side and each with its justification. For it is not by insisting on one of these tones, but by letting them sound together, that one arrives at the truth. And just as our intimate corporeal relation with Sun, Moon and Earth is placed in the midst of the seven planets, so Anthropomorphism is the world-outlook nearest to the harmony that can sound forth from Theism, Intuitionism and Naturalism, while this harmony again is closest to the conjoined effect of the seven psychic moods; and these seven moods are shaded according to the twelve signs of the Zodiac.

You see, it is not true to talk in terms of one cosmic conception, but of

$$12 + 7 = 19 + 3 = 22 + 1 = 23$$

cosmic conceptions which all have their justification. We have twenty-three legitimate names for cosmic conceptions. But all the rest can arise from the fact that the corresponding planets pass through the twelve spiritual signs of the encircling Zodiac. And now try, from what has been explained, to enter into the task confronting Spiritual Science: the task of acting as peacemaker among the various world-outlooks. The way to peace is to realise that the world-outlooks conjointly, in their reciprocal action on one another, can be in a certain sense explained, but that they cannot lead into the inner nature of truth if they remain one-sided. One must experience in oneself the truth-value of the different world-outlooks, in order—if one may say so—to be in agreement with truth. Just as you can picture to yourselves the physical cosmos; the Zodiac, the planetary system; Sun, Moon and Earth (the three together) and the Earth on its own account, so you can think of a spiritual universe: Anthropomorphism; Theism, Intuitionism, Naturalism; Gnosis, Logicism, Voluntarism, Empiricism, Mysticism, Transcendentalism, Occultism, and all this moving round through the twelve spiritual Zodiacal signs. All this does exist, only it exists spiritually. As truly as the physical cosmos exists physically, so truly does this other universe exist spiritually.

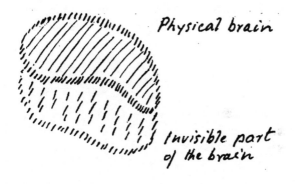

Physical brain

Invisible part of the brain

In that half of the brain which is found by the anatomist, and of which one may say that it is shaped like a half-hemisphere, those activities of the spiritual cosmos which proceed from the upper nuances are specially operative. On the other hand, there is a part of the brain which is visible only when one observes the etheric body; and this is specially influenced by the lower part of the spiritual cosmos. (Diagrams, pp. 39 and 50.) But how is it with this influencing? Let us say of someone that with his Logicism he is placed in Sensationalism, and that with his Empiricism he is placed in Mathematism. The resulting forces then work into his brain, so that the upper part of his brain is specially active and dominates the rest. Countless varieties of brain-activity arise from the fact that the brain swims, as it were, in the spiritual cosmos, and its forces work into the brain in the way we have been able to describe. The brains of men are as varied in kind as all the possible combinations that can spring from this spiritual cosmos. The lower part of the spiritual cosmos does not act on the physical brain at all, but on the etheric brain.

The best impression one can retain from the whole subject would lead one to say: It opens out for me a feeling for the immensity of the world, for the qualitatively sublime in the world, for the possibility that man can exist in endless variety in this world. Truly, if we consider only this, we can already say to ourselves: There is no lack of varied possibilities open to us for the different incarnations that we have to go through on earth. And one can also feel sure that anyone who looks at the world in this light will be impelled to say: "Ah, how grand, how rich, the world is! What happiness it is to go on and on taking part, in ways ever more varied, in its existence, its activities, its endeavours!"

LECTURE FOUR

WE HAVE been concerned with the possible varieties of world-outlooks, of world-outlook-moods and so on, which can find place in the human soul, and since I can take only single points of view from this wide field, I should like to illustrate one of these points of view by means of a special example.

Let us suppose that a person so lives in the world that among his natural predispositions we find the special forces through which he is influenced by the world-outlook of Idealism. We will say that he makes this world-outlook into a dominating factor in his inner life, so that the soul-mood which I designated yesterday as Mysticism, and called the Venus mood, flows towards Idealism and is nourished by its powers. Hence, if one speaks in the symbols of astrology, one would say that the spiritual constellation of such a man, according to his natural predispositions, is that Venus stands in Aries.

I remark expressly, so that no misunderstanding may arise, that these constellations are of much greater importance in the life of the person than the constellations of the external horoscope, and do not necessarily coincide with the "nativity"—the external horoscope. For the enhanced influence which is exerted on the soul by this standing of Mysticism in the sign of Idealism waits for the propitious moment when it can lay hold of the soul most fruitfully. Such influences need not assert themselves just at the time of birth; they can do so before birth, or after it. In short, they await the point of time when these predispositions can best be built into the human organism, according to its inner configuration.

Hence the ordinary astrological "nativity" does not come into account here. But one can say: A certain soul is by nature such that, spiritually speaking, Venus stands in Aries—Mysticism in

57

the sign of Idealism. Now the forces which arise in this way do not remain constant throughout life. They change—that is, the person comes under other influences, under other spiritual signs and also under other moods of soul. Let us suppose that a man so changes that in the course of his life he comes into the soul-mood of Empiricism; that Mysticism has moved on, as it were, into Empiricism, and Empiricism stands in the sign of Rationalism. You see, as I drew it in the preceding lecture, going from inwards outwards in the symbolic picture, that Empiricism stands in relation to Mysticism as does the Sun to Venus. With regard to its mood the soul has progressed to Empiricism and has at the same time placed itself in the sign of Rationalism. The result is that such a soul changes its world-picture. What the soul formerly produced, perhaps as a specially strong personality in the time when in its case Mysticism stood in the sign of Idealism, this will pass over into another nuance of world-outlook. What the soul asserts and says will be different when in this way its world-outlook-mood has passed over from Mysticism to Empiricism, and the latter has placed itself in the sign of Rationalism. However, from what I have now explained, you can gather that human souls can have an inclination to change the sign and mood of their world-outlook. (See p. 50.) For these souls the tendency to change is already given. Let us suppose that such a soul wants to carry this tendency further in life. It wants to swing forward from Empiricism to the next soul-mood, i.e. to Voluntarism; and if it wants to swing forward also in the zodiacal signs, then it will come into Mathematism. It would then pass over to a world-outlook which in this symbolical picture leads away at an angle of 60° from the first line, where Mysticism stood in the sign of Idealism; and such a soul, in the course of the same incarnation, would bring to expression a mathematical world-structure permeated by and based upon the will.

And now I ask you to notice how I work out this matter. It will be seen that two such constellations as are here present in the soul disturb each other in the course of time; they influence each other unfavourably when they are at an angle of 60° with regard to each other. In physical astrology this is a favourable constellation;

in spiritual astrology this so-called sextile aspect is unfavourable. We can see this because this last position—Voluntarism in Mathematism—comes up against a severe hindrance in the soul. The soul is not able to develop, because it cannot find anything to lay hold of, since the person in question has no natural gift for Mathematism.

This is how the unfavourable character of the sextile aspect expresses itself. Hence this configuration, Voluntarism in the sign of Mathematism, cannot establish itself. The consequence is that the soul does not try to move forward in this way. But because it cannot take the path to Voluntarism in Mathematism, it turns away from the configuration it now has—Empiricism in Rationalism—and seeks an outlet by placing itself in opposition to the direction it cannot take. Such a soul, accordingly, would not swing forward to Voluntarism in the direction of Mathematism, but would place itself with Voluntarism in opposition to its Empiricism. The result is that Voluntarism would stand in opposition to Rationalism in the sign of Dynamism. And in the course of its life, such a soul would have as its possible configuration one in which it would defend a world-outlook based on a special pressing in of forces, of Dynamism permeated by will—a will that wants to effect its purpose by force. In spiritual astrology things are again different from what they are in physical astrology; in physical astrology "opposition" has a quite different significance. Here, "opposition" is brought about by the soul

59

being unable to proceed further along an unfavourable path; it veers round into the opposing configuration.

I have shown you here what the soul of Nietzsche went through in the course of his life. If you try to understand the course he takes in his early works, you will find that the placing of Mysticism makes it comprehensible. From this period we have "The Birth of Tragedy"; "David Strauss, the Confessor and the Writer"; "The Use and Abuse of History"; "Schopenhauer as Educator"; "Richard Wagner in Bayreuth". Then the soul of Nietzsche moves on; a second epoch begins. Here we find "Human, all too Human"; "The Dawn of Day"; "The Joyful Wisdom"—all proceeding from the oppositional configuration. These are writings based on the will to power, on the will saturated with force, with power.

Thus you see how an inner conformity to law exists between the spiritual cosmos and the way in which man stands within it. If we employ the symbols of astrology, but taking them to express something different, we can say: In the case of Nietzsche, up to a certain time in his life Venus stood in Aries, but when for his soul this configuration passed over into "Sun in the sign of Taurus", he could get no further. He could not go with Mars into the sign of Gemini, but went into the oppositional position; thus he went with Mars into the sign of Scorpio. His last phase was characterised by his standing with Mars in Scorpio. But one can sustain this configuration only if one penetrates into the lower position (below the line Idealism—Realism in the [diagram on p. 50) where one plunges into a spiritual world-outlook, Occultism or something similar; otherwise these configurations must work back unfavourably upon the person himself. Hence the tragic fate of Nietzsche. One can go through with the upper configurations if one is able, owing to external circumstances, to place oneself in the world in a corresponding way. The configurations below the line from Idealism to Realism can be sustained only if one dives down into the spiritual world—a thing that Nietzsche could not do. By "placing oneself externally in the world" I mean placing by means of education, by means of external conditions; they come into account for all that lies above the line running from Idealism to Realism. Meditative life, a life devoted to the study and understanding of Spiritual Science, comes into account for all that lies below the line.

In order to grasp the importance of what has been sketched out in these lectures, we must know the following things. We must make it clear to ourselves what thinking really is; how it enters into human experience.

The uncompromising materialist of our day finds it suits his purpose to say that the brain forms the thought—more exactly, that the central nervous system forms the thought. For anyone who sees through things, this is about as true as to say when one looks into a mirror that the mirror has "made" the face. In fact, the face is outside the mirror; the mirror only reflects the face, throws it back. The experience a man has of his thoughts is quite similar. (We will leave aside for the moment other aspects of the soul.) The experience of real, active thinking no more arises from the brain than the image of a face is created by the mirror. The brain, in fact, works only as a reflecting apparatus, whereby it throws back the soul-activity and this becomes visible to itself. The brain has as little to do with what a man perceives as thoughts as a mirror has to do with your face when you see it in a glass. But there is something more than that. When someone thinks, he really perceives only the last phases of his thinking-activity, of his thinking experience. And now, in order to make this clear, I want to take up once more the comparison with the mirror.

Imagine that you are standing there and want to see your face in a mirror. If you have no mirror, then you cannot see your face. You may look as long as you like, but you will not see your face. If you want to see it, you must work up some material so that it reflects your face. That is, you must first prepare the material so that it can produce the reflection. Then, when you gaze at the surface, you see your face. The soul has to do the same with the brain. The actual perceiving of a thought is preceded by a thinking activity that works upon the brain. For example, if you want to perceive the thought "lion", your thinking activity first sets in motion certain parts of the brain, deep within it, so that they become the "mirror" for the perception of the thought "lion". And the agent who thus makes the brain into a mirror is you yourself. What you finally perceive as thoughts are the reflections, the mirror-pictures; what you first have to prepare so that the right reflection may appear is some part or other of the brain. You, with your soul-activity, are the very thing that gives the brain the form and capacity for reflecting your thinking as thoughts. If you want to go back to the activity on which the thought is based, then it is the activity which, from out of the soul, takes hold of the brain and gets to work there. And when from out of your soul you set up a certain activity in your brain, this brings about a reflection such that you perceive the thought "lion". You see, a soul-spiritual element has to be there first. Then, through its activity, the brain is made into a mirror-like apparatus for reflecting the thought. That is the real process, but such a muddled idea of it prevails that many people nowadays cannot grasp it at all.

A person who makes a little progress in occult perception can separate the two phases of his soul-activity. He can trace how it is that when he wants to think something or other, he has first not simply to grasp the thought, but to prepare his brain for it. If he has prepared it so that it reflects, then he has the thought. When one wants to investigate occultly, so that one can picture things, one always has, first, the task of carrying through the activity which prepares the picturing. It is this that is so important for us to notice. For it is only when we keep these things well in mind that we have before us the real activity of human thinking. Now for the first time we know how human thinking-activity is carried out. First, this activity lays hold of the brain, in connection somewhere with the central nervous system. It sets in motion— let us say if we wish—the atomistic portions in some way, brings them into some sort of movement; by this means they become a mirror-apparatus; the *thought* is reflected, and the soul becomes conscious of the *thought*. Thus we have to distinguish two phases: first the work on the brain from out of the psychic-spiritual in preparation for the external physical experience; then the perception takes place, after the work on the brain has prepared the ground for this act of perceiving by the soul. In the ordinary way this preparatory work on the brain remains entirely unconscious. But an occult researcher must start by actually experiencing it. He has to go through the experience of how the soul-activity is poured in, and the brain made ready to reflect the thought as an image.

What I have now explained happens continually to a person between waking up and going to sleep. The thinking activity is always working on the brain, and so, throughout the waking state, it makes the brain into a mirror-apparatus for the thoughts. But it is not sufficient that the only thinking-activity worked up in us should be that worked up by ourselves. For one might say it is a narrowly limited activity that is here worked up in this way by means of the psychic-spiritual. When we wake up in the morning and are awake through the day, and in the evening fall asleep again, then the psychic-spiritual activity which belongs to the thinking is working all day long upon the brain, and thereby the brain becomes a reflecting-apparatus. But the brain must first be there; then the soul-spiritual activity can make little furrows in the brain, or, one might say, its memoranda and engravings. The main substance and form of the brain must first be there. But that is not enough for our human life.

Our brain could not be worked upon by our daily life if our whole organism were not so prepared that it provides a basis for this daily work. And this work of preparation comes from the cosmos. Thus as we work daily at the "engraving" of the brain, which makes it into a mirror-apparatus for our daily thoughts, so, in so far as we cannot ourselves do this engraving, this giving form, form has to be given to us from the cosmos. As our little thoughts work and make their little engravings, so must our whole organism be built up from out of the cosmos, according to the same pattern of thought-activity. For example, that which appears to us finally in the sign of Idealism is present in the spiritual cosmos as the activity producing Idealism, and it can so work upon a man that it prepares his whole organism so that he inclines to Idealism. In like manner are the other varieties of moods and signs worked in upon men from out of the spiritual cosmos.

Man is built up according to the thoughts of the cosmos. The cosmos is the "great thinker" which down to our last finger-nail engraves our form in us, just as our little thought-work makes its little imprints on our brain every day. As our brain—I am referring only to the small portions where imprints can be made—stands under the influence of the work of thinking, so does the whole man stand under the influence of cosmic thinking.

Take the example I gave you, the example of Nietzsche—what does it mean? It means that through an earlier incarnation Nietzsche was so prepared in his karma that at a certain point of time, by virtue of his earlier incarnation, the forces of Idealism and of Mysticism (working together because Mysticism stood in the sign of Idealism) so worked upon his whole bodily constitution that he was in the first place capable of becoming a mystical Idealist. Then his constellation altered in the way indicated.

We are thought out from the cosmos—the cosmos thinks us. And just as we, in our little daily thought-work, make little engravings in our brain, and then the ideas "lion", "dog," "table", "rose", "book", "on", "right", "left", come into our consciousness as reflections of that which we have prepared in our brain—i.e. just as we, through the working-up of the brain, finally perceive, lion, dog, table, rose, book, on, off, right, write, read —the Beings of the cosmic Hierarchies work in such a way that they carry out the great thought-activity which engraves upon the world things far more significant than our daily thought-activity can accomplish. So it comes to pass that not only the tiny little markings arise and are then reflected singly as our thoughts, but that we ourselves, in our whole being, appear again to the Beings of the higher Hierarchies as their thoughts. As our little brain-processes mirror our little thoughts, so do we mirror the thoughts of the cosmos which are engraved upon the world. When the Hierarchies of the cosmos "think", they "think", for example, men. As our little thoughts emerge from our little brain-processes, so do the thoughts of the Hierarchies arise from their work, to which we ourselves belong. As parts of our brain are for us the reflecting-apparatus which we first work up for our thoughts, so are we, we little beings, the substance which the Hierarchies of the cosmos prepare for their thoughts. Thus we might say, in a certain sense, that we can feel ourselves with regard to the cosmos as a little portion of our brain might feel with regard to ourselves. But as little as we, in our soul-spiritual nature, are our brains, so little are the Beings of the Hierarchies "we". Hence we have an independent status in relation to the Beings of the higher Hierarchies. And we can say that while in a certain manner we serve them so that they may be able to think through us, yet at the same time we are independent beings with identities of our own, as indeed, in a certain way, the particles of our brain have their own life.

Thus we find the connection between human and cosmic thoughts. Human thought is the regent of the brain; cosmic thought is such a regent that we belong with our whole being to that which it has to accomplish. Only, because in consequence of our karma it cannot direct its thoughts on to us all equally, we have to be constituted in accordance with its logic. Thus we men have a logic according to which we think, and so have the Spiritual Hierarchies of the cosmos their logic. And their logic was indicated in the diagram I drew for you (see lecture three, p. 50). As when we think, for example, "The lion is a mammal", we bring two concepts together to make a statement, so the Spiritual Hierarchies of the cosmos think two things together, Mysticism and Idealism, and we then say: "Mysticism appears in Idealism." Imagine this first as the preparatory activity of the cosmos. Then resounds the Creative Fiat, the Creative Word. For the Beings of the Spiritual Hierarchies the preparatory act consists in the choice of a human being whose karma is such that he can develop a natural bent for becoming a mystical Idealist. Into the Hierarchies of the cosmos there is rayed back something that we should call a "thought", whereas for them it is the expression of a man who is a mystical Idealist. He is their "thought", after they have prepared for themselves the cosmic decision—"Let Mysticism appear in Idealism."

We have now, in a certain sense, depicted the inner aspect of the Cosmic Word, of Cosmic Thought. What we drew in a diagram as "cosmic logic" represents how the Spiritual Hierarchies of the cosmos think. For example: "Let Empiricism appear in the sign of Rationalism!" and so on. Let us try to realise what can be thought in the cosmos in this way. It can be thought: "Let Mysticism appear in the sign of Idealism! Let it change! Let it become Empiricism in the sign of Rationalism!" Opposition! The next move on would represent a false cosmic decision. After verification, the thought is changed round. The third standpoint must appear: "Voluntarism in the sign of Dynamism." These three decisions, through being spoken over a period in the cosmic worlds, give the "man Nietzsche". And he rays back as the thought of the cosmos.

Thus does the collectivity of the Hierarchies speak in the cosmos! And our human thinking-activity is a copy, a tiny copy, of it.

Worlds are related to the Spirit or to the Spirits of the cosmos as our brain is to our soul. Thus we may have a glimpse into something which we ought certainly to look upon only with a certain reverence, with a holy awe. For in contemplating it we stand before the mysteries of human individuality. We learn to understand—if I may express myself figuratively—that the eyes of the Beings of the higher Hierarchies roam over the single individualities among men, and that the individuals are to them what the individual letters of a book are to us when we are reading. This we may look upon only with holy awe: we are overhearing the thought-activity of the cosmos.

In our day the veil over such a mystery as this must be lifted to a certain degree; for the laws which have here been shown as the laws of the thinking of the cosmos are active in man. And the knowledge of them can help us to understand life, and then to understand ourselves; so that even when, for one reason or another, we have to be placed one-sidedly in life, we know that we belong to a great whole, for we are links in the thought-logic of the cosmos. And in learning to grasp these relations, Spiritual Science acts as our guide. It teaches us to understand our one-sided predispositions as much as it enlarges our all-round knowledge. Thus we can find the frame of mind which is necessary precisely in our time. For to-day, when in many leading minds there is no trace of insight into the relationships we have touched on here, we experience the effects of these relations or connections but do not know how to live under them. And thus they create conditions which call for adjustment.

Let us take the example of Wundt, whom I mentioned yesterday. His one-sidedness is brought about through a quite definite constellation. Let us suppose that he could ever struggle on to an understanding of Spiritual Science, then he would look upon his one-sidedness in such a way that he would say to himself: "Now because I stand here with my Empiricism, etc., I am in a position to do good work in certain fields. I will remain in these, and will make up for it in other ways through Spiritual Science." To such a decision as this he would come. But he refuses to know anything about Spiritual Science. What does he do in consequence? Whereas he could carry out something good and productive in the constellation which is his, he turns what lies within his range into a complete philosophy. Otherwise he could probably do something greater, much greater; indeed he would be most useful if he would leave philosophising alone and go in for experimental psychology—a thing he understands—and if he would inquire into the nature of mathematical conclusions—which he also understands—instead of making a concoction of all kinds of philosophy; for then he would be on the right lines.

But this must be said of many. Therefore Spiritual Science, while it must evoke the feeling by which we recognise how there should be peace between world-outlooks, must also point sharply to cases where persons go beyond the necessary limits set for them by their constellations. These persons do great harm by hypnotising the world with opinions that get by without any attention being paid to the constellation behind them. All forms of one-sidedness that try to claim universal validity must be strongly repulsed. The world does not admit of being explained by a person who has special predilections for this or that. And when he wants to explain it on his own and so to found a philosophy, then this philosophy works harmfully, and Spiritual Science has the task of rejecting the arrogance of this pretentious claim to universality. In our time, the less feeling there is for Spiritual Science, the more strongly will this one-sidedness appear. Hence we see that knowledge of the nature of human and cosmic thought can lead us to understand rightly the significance and the task of Spiritual Science, and to see how it can bring into a right relationship other so-called spiritual streams, especially philosophic currents, in our time. It must be wished that knowledge of the kind that we have tried to bring together for ourselves in these four lectures should inscribe itself deeply into the hearts and souls of our friends, so that the course of the anthroposophical spiritual stream through the world should take a quite definite and right direction. It would thereby be recognised more and more how a man is formed through that which lives in him as cosmic thought.

With the aid of such an explanation as this we see more depth that we could otherwise do in a thought of Fichte's, where he says: "What kind of a philosophy a man has depends on the kind of man he is." Yes, indeed, the kind of philosophy a man has does verily depend on the kind of man he is! The fact that Fichte (in the first period of the incarnation he was then living through as Fichte) could say, as the basic nerve of his philosophy of life: "Our world is the sensualised material of our duty" [see footnote, p. 32], shows even as does the previously quoted saying (which he gave out later) how his soul changed its constellation in the spiritual cosmos. That is, it shows how richly this soul was endowed, so that the spiritual Hierarchies could remould it so that through it they could think various things for themselves. Something similar could be said of Nietzsche, for example.

Many different ways of viewing the world emerge if one keeps before one's soul such things as have been described in these four lectures. The best we can gain from these descriptions is that with their aid we should come to look ever more and more deeply, with perceptive feeling, into the spiritual features of the world.

If only one thing were to be achieved by means of such a lecture-course as this, it would be that as many as possible of you should say to yourselves: "Yes, if anyone wants to enter into the spiritual world—i.e. into the world of Truth, and not into the world of error—he must really set out upon the path! For much, much must be taken into consideration along this path in order to come to the sources of truth. And if at the beginning it might

68

seem to me as if a contradiction appears here or there, if in one place or another I could not understand something, I will still say to myself that the world is not there in order to be grasped by every condition of human understanding, and that I would rather be a seeker than a man whose sole attitude towards the world is such that he only enquires 'What can I understand?' 'What can I not understand?' "

If one becomes a seeker, if one earnestly sets to work along the path of the seeker, then one learns to know that one must bring together impulses from the most varied sides in order to gain an understanding of the world. And then one unlearns every kind of attitude towards the world that asks "Do I understand that?" "Do I not understand that?", and instead one seeks and seeks and goes on seeking. The worst enemies of truth are cosmic conceptions that are exclusive and strive after finality; the conceptions of those who want to frame a couple of thoughts and suppose that with them they can dare to build up a world-edifice.

The world is boundless, both qualitatively and quantitatively. And it will be a blessing when there are individual souls who wish for clear vision with regard to that which is appearing in our day with such terrible overweening narrow-mindedness, and wants to be "universal". I might say: "With bleeding heart I declare that the greatest hindrance to knowledge of how a preparatory work of thought-activity is carried out in the brain, how the brain is thereby made into a mirror and the life of the soul reflected from it—a fact which could throw endless light on much other physiological knowledge—the greatest hindrance to the knowledge of this fact is the crazy modern physiology which speaks of two kinds of nerves, the 'motor' and the 'sensory' nerves." (I have touched on this in many lectures already.) In order to produce this theory, which crops up everywhere in physiology, it is a fact that physiology had first to lose all understanding. Hence it is a theory now recognised all over the earth, and it acts as a hindrance to all true knowledge of the nature of thought and the nature of the soul. Never will it be possible to understand human thought if physiology sets up such an obstacle to true knowledge. But things have gone so far that an indefensible physiology forms the introduction to every textbook of psychology and teaching about the mind, and makes it dependent on this falsity. Therewith the door is bolted also against knowledge of cosmic thought.

One first learns to recognise what thought is in the cosmos when one comes to feel what human thinking is: that in its true nature it has nothing to do with the brain except that it is the master of the brain. But when one has thus recognised thought in its essence, when one has come to know oneself in thinking, then one feels oneself inwardly within the cosmic, and our knowledge of the true nature of cosmic thought. When we learn to know rightly what our thinking is, then we learn also to know how we are "thought" by the Powers of the cosmos. Indeed we may gain a glimpse into the logic of the Hierarchies. The single components of the decisions of the Hierarchies, the concepts of the Hierarchies, I have written down for you. In the twelve spiritual signs of the Zodiac, in the seven world-outlook-moods, and so on, lie the concepts of the Hierarchies; and human beings are constituted in accordance with the verdicts of the cosmos which result from these concepts. Thus we feel ourselves within the logic of the cosmos—that is (if we really grasp it) within the logic of the Hierarchies of the cosmos. We feel ourselves as souls embedded in cosmic thought, just as we feel our thoughts, the little thoughts we think, embedded in our soul-life.

Meditate sometimes on the ideas: "I think my thoughts," and "I am a thought which is thought by the Hierarchies of the cosmos." My eternal part consists in this—that the thought of the Hierarchies is eternal. And when I have once been thought out by one category of the Hierarchies, then I am passed on—as a human thought is passed on from teacher to pupil—from one category to another, so that this in turn may think me in my true, eternal nature. Thus I feel myself within the thought-world of the cosmos.

Note on Rudolf Steiner's Lectures

The lectures and addresses contained in this volume have been translated from the German, which is based on stenographic and other recorded texts that were in most cases never seen or revised by the lecturer. Hence, due to human errors in hearing and transcription, they may contain mistakes and faulty passages. Every effort has been made to ensure that this is not the case. Some of the lectures were given to audiences more familiar with anthroposophy; these are the so-called 'private' or 'members' lectures. Other lectures, like the written works, were intended for the general public. The difference between these, as Rudolf Steiner indicates in his *Autobiography*, is twofold. On the one hand, the members' lectures take for granted a background in and commitment to anthroposophy; in the public lectures this was not the case. At the same time, the members' lectures address the concerns and dilemmas of the members, while the public work arises from, and directly addresses Steiner's own understanding of universal needs. Nevertheless, as Rudolf Steiner stresses: 'Nothing was ever said that was not solely the result of my direct experience of the growing content of anthroposophy. There was never any question of concessions to the prejudices and preferences of the members. Whoever reads these privately printed lectures can take them to represent anthroposophy in the fullest sense. Thus it was possible without hesitation—when the complaints in this direction became too persistent—to depart from the custom of circulating this material "For members only". But it must be borne in mind that faulty passages do occur in these reports not revised by myself.' Earlier in the same chapter, he states: 'Had I been able to correct them [*the private lectures*], the restriction *for members only* would have been unnecessary from the beginning.' The original German editions on which this text is based were published by Rudolf Steiner Verlag, Dornach, Switzerland in the collected edition

(*Gesamtausgabe*, 'GA') of Rudolf Steiner's work. All publications are edited by the Rudolf Steiner Nachlassverwaltung (estate), which wholly owns both Rudolf Steiner Verlag and the Rudolf Steiner Archive.